SØREN STAUN PETERSEN

RHUBARB

NEW AND CLASSIC RECIPES FOR SWEET AND SAVORY DISHES

TOUCHWOOD

CONTENTS

PREFACE

Rhubarb. A true harbinger of spring. With its long red stems and large green crowns, rhubarb is not to be overlooked. But don't we perhaps have preconceived notions about its role in the kitchen? Sure, it's brilliant in desserts and sweet things, but can it do more? I have completely immersed myself in rhubarb and have pushed it to the limit to determine just how much it can be used for. In this book, you'll find out just how versatile rhubarb is. It can do much more than you think.

Trifles, porridge, jam, and soup. This is the extent of most people's familiarity with rhubarb in cooking. But what if I say risotto, baked salmon, or pizza? These are not things that you immediately think of when you think of rhubarb, but actually they go immensely well with rhubarb's acidity and light sweetness.

Back in the day, rhubarb became popular because it filled a gap in the season. It was the first "fruit" of the year that could be harvested. And in early spring, people hungered for something tart and sweet. Unfortunately, when we started importing fruit from hot countries, rhubarb was forgotten—suddenly, we could get apples, pears, etc. all year round.

This cookbook provides new and different ways to use rhubarb both in savory and sweet iterations—for example, added to quinoa, and as a fresh yet tart addition to a pulled pork burger. It also takes you through all the classic recipes such as rhubarb pie—but with twists you may not have seen before.

Rhubarb lends itself wonderfully to preserves such as compotes and juices, and so you will also find chapters with a base recipe and then several different recipes that use this base. After all, the rhubarb season is short, and preserving it provides an opportunity to enjoy the taste for much longer. I hope the recipes within this book will inspire you.

Søren Staun Petersen

INTRODUCTION

This book is divided into two main parts. In the first half, we use fresh rhubarb. In the second part, we make compote, relish/chutney, and juice—and then make dishes with these. Both parts contain savory and sweet recipes. Some recipes are classic, familiar dishes, and some include new, exciting ways to use rhubarb.

VARIETIES

In North America, you can find several varieties of rhubarb, but they can generally be classified into two types: green and red. Among the green types, there is one cultivar that is by far the most common: Victoria, which gives a high yield for the gardener. It is sour in taste and is not red all the way through the stem. This variety is robust, large, and easy to grow. It is pest and disease resistant, making it the most favored.

There are many varieties of red rhubarb including Colorado Red and Chipman's Canada Red. This type of rhubarb is quite a bit smaller and is completely red through the stem. It can be a little harder to find, but it's the one that has the most flavor and is a little sweeter.

SEASON

Rhubarb has a primary season that goes from late April to late June. However, due to high demand, a second season has emerged that spans August to September.

OTHER

All recipes are for 4 people, unless otherwise stated.
All recipes are made in a convection oven, unless otherwise stated.
In all recipes, the rhubarb must, of course, be washed thoroughly before use.

RHUBARB: A HUMBLE VEGETABLE

We probably don't think of rhubarb as a vegetable, but it is, biologically speaking. However, it is hardly as useful in everyday cooking as, for example, root vegetables and cabbage.

Of the health-promoting properties, rhubarb's high dietary fiber content should be highlighted: 3.8 grams of dietary fiber per 100 grams, which places it in the group of vegetables with high dietary fiber content. The fiber content helps to give us a feeling of satiety. The healthy dietary fiber that rhubarb contains has been used medicinally, namely as a remedy for digestive problems—not least constipation.

From a nutritional perspective, rhubarb contributes a modest amount of energy, just 26 kilocalories per 100 grams. For comparison, carrot contains 38 kilocalories per 100 grams.

Moreover, you also get a great variety of nutrients from rhubarb; these include vitamin C, potassium, calcium, and antioxidants. The red color of the stems is due to the high content of anthocyanins, the same antioxidant typically found in dark berries.

The rough sensation you might feel on your tongue and teeth when enjoying rhubarb is due to the content of oxalic acid. The oxalic acid binds and prevents lime from draining into the bloodstream, but it is neutralized when consumed with calcium-containing foods (e.g., dairy products).

Cathrine Ilsøe, clinical dietitian and advisor on diet and lifestyle

THE SAVORY

SPRING POTATO SALAD

1 cup cubed rhubarb
3 Tbsp cane sugar
1½ lb potatoes, boiled and cooled
⅔ cup 18% crème fraiche
1 cup mayonnaise
2 tsp Dijon mustard
Salt and pepper, to taste
1 small red onion
Fresh chives
Lime juice, to taste

Put the cubed rhubarb into a saucepan. Add the sugar and ¼ cup of water and let simmer. The cubes should be a little tender, but it is important that they do not overcook—there should still be a bite to them. Drain and let them cool.

Cut the potatoes into large or small pieces, depending on your preference.

Mix together the crème fraiche, mayonnaise, and Dijon. Season with a little salt and pepper. Finely chop the red onion and chives and mix them into the dressing.

Finally, stir in the potatoes, rhubarb, and lime juice.

PIZZA BIANCA

DOUGH
3 tsp active dry yeast
⅔ cup lukewarm water
1 Tbsp olive oil
1¾ cups pizza flour (ordinary wheat flour can be used)
Pinch of salt

TOPPINGS
4 small potatoes
5 stalks rhubarb
3 oz cured chorizo sausage
1 cup aged cheddar
1 cup ricotta

Stir the yeast into the water. Add the other ingredients and knead the dough thoroughly. Let the dough rise to double its size, about 1 hour.

Preheat oven to 475°F.

Cut the potatoes into very thin slices. Cut the rhubarb and chorizo into thin slices. Grate the cheddar and mix with the ricotta.

Divide the dough into two balls and roll out. Top each pizza with the cheese, potatoes, rhubarb, and chorizo.

Bake for 20–25 minutes.

RISOTTO WITH HAKE

5 stalks rhubarb
⅓ cup olive oil + more
   for greasing pans
2 onions
2½ cups arborio rice
⅔ cup white wine
6 cups vegetable broth (approx.)

⅓ cup butter + more for frying
⅓ cup Parmesan, grated
4 hake fillets, each about 4 oz
Salt and pepper
Fresh parsley

Preheat oven to 375°F.

Cut the rhubarb in half lengthwise, or into several pieces if the stems are thick. Grease a dish with olive oil, add the rhubarb, drizzle with more olive oil, and add a sprinkle of salt. Bake for 25 minutes.

Dice the onion. In a large pan over medium-high heat, add the ⅓ cup olive oil, the onion and rice. Stir until the rice becomes clear, about 4 minutes. Pour the wine into the rice mixture and bring to a boil. Cook, until almost evaporated. Reduce heat to medium and pour ½ cup of the broth into the pan and cook, stirring gently until broth is absorbed. Continue to cook, adding about ½ cup of broth at at time, and stirring until broth is absorbed before adding more, until the rice is al dente, about 20 minutes.

When all the broth has been added and absorbed, add the butter, parmesan, and rhubarb and gently stir.

Score the hake fillets a couple of times on the skin side and fry, skin side down, over high heat in a bit of oil for 2–3 minutes. Turn down the heat and continue to fry until the meat has turned white. Add some butter to the pan, let it simmer, and fry the fish on the other side for 10 seconds. Season with salt and pepper.

Garnish the dish with a sprinkle of parsley.

Note: You can replace hake with any firm white fish such as cod, tilapia, or halibut.

PORK CUTLETS WITH SPICED RHUBARB QUINOA

QUINOA

2 small red onions
2 cloves garlic
4 stalks rhubarb
⅔ cup quinoa
1¼ cup water
⅔ cup cream
Juice and zest of 1 orange
1 tsp ground ginger
1 Tbsp sugar
A little grated nutmeg
Salt and pepper

PORK CUTLETS

5 rashers smoked bacon
4 pork tenderloin cutlets
Butter for frying
Salt and pepper

Preheat oven to 375°F. Grease an ovenproof 2-quart casserole dish.

Dice the red onion, garlic, and rhubarb, and add to a large bowl. Add the quinoa, water, cream, orange juice and zest, ginger, sugar, nutmeg, and salt and pepper to the same bowl, and stir to combine. Place mixture in greased ovenproof dish and bake for 30 minutes.

Place the bacon in a pan and fry until almost crispy. Remove the bacon and set aside, leaving the fat in the pan.

While the quinoa dish is still baking, fry the cutlets in the bacon fat and a little butter, and season with salt and pepper. They only need about 30 seconds on each side.

Place the bacon and cutlets in the quinoa dish and continue to bake for 10 minutes. If the dish seems dry, add more water while it finishes baking.

SWEET AND SOUR WOK

WOK

1 lb sirloin, tenderloin,
    or top shoulder blade steak
2 Tbsp five-spice
7 oz egg noodles
1 red bell pepper
2 large carrots
4 stalks lemongrass
1½ cups broccolini florets
2 stalks rhubarb
Sesame oil for frying
¾ cup snap peas
1 cup shelled edamame beans

SAUCE

2 tsp cornstarch
4 Tbsp water
3 Tbsp rhubarb juice
    (or brine from pineapple)
2 Tbsp rice vinegar/
    white wine vinegar
1 Tbsp sugar
2 Tbsp ketchup
1 Tbsp soy sauce
½ Tbsp chili sauce

GARNISH

½ bunch spring onions, sliced
Cashews or peanuts (optional)

Cut the beef into strips and rub it thoroughly with the five-spice.

To make the sauce, stir together the cornstarch and water in a bowl. In another bowl mix the remaining ingredients for the sauce. Set both bowls aside.

Boil the noodles. Cut the bell pepper, carrots, lemongrass, broccolini, and rhubarb into thin strips.

Set a pan on high heat and add the sesame oil. Add the beef and fry it for 1 minute. Then add the bell pepper, carrots, and lemongrass and fry for another 2 minutes. Finally, add the broccolini, rhubarb, snap peas, and edamame beans. Fry it all for another minute. Add the sauce and the cornstarch mixture and combine.

Serve with the noodles, and top with the spring onions, and (optionally) cashews or peanuts.

CHICKEN WITH PEARL BARLEY

5 oz bacon
1 small handful fresh mint, or to taste
1 small handful fresh chives, or to taste
2 chicken breasts
A little oil for frying
2 stalks rhubarb
1 onion
1¼ cups pearl barley
2 tsp ground ginger
1¼ cups + 3 Tbsp white wine
1½ cups vegetable broth
⅓ cup cream
Salt and pepper

Cut the bacon into cubes and fry in a pan until crispy. Roughly chop the mint and chives and mix with the bacon. Set aside.

Cut the chicken breasts into smaller pieces and sauté briefly in a large pan with a bit of oil over high heat, until they acquire a crust.

Cut the rhubarb into 1½ inch pieces. Peel the onion, then halve and cut into thin slices. Put the pan on medium heat and add the rhubarb, onion, pearl barley, and ground ginger, and sauté briefly.

Add the white wine and reduce for 10 minutes. Add the broth and cook for another 15 minutes. Add the cream and let simmer until combined. Season with salt and pepper.

Sprinkle the bacon and herbs over the finished pearl barley and serve the dish immediately.

SALMON WITH CABBAGE AND RHUBARB

1 Tbsp mustard seeds

1 Tbsp cumin seeds

1 Tbsp fennel seeds

3 stalks rhubarb

1¼ cups orange juice

3 Tbsp water

⅔ cup cane sugar

3 Tbsp fresh ginger cut
    into small pieces

⅓ cup white wine

⅓ cup white wine vinegar

½ head savoy cabbage,
    cut into strips

1⅓ cups black rice

4 pieces salmon

Olive oil

Salt and pepper

A few spoonfuls of crème fraiche

Toast all seeds in a pan until they pop. Remove from heat and set aside.

Cut the rhubarb into long matchstick-thin strips.

Boil the orange juice, water, and sugar in a saucepan. When the sugar is dissolved, add the seeds and the ginger. Simmer to a syrup over medium heat for about 10 minutes. Add the rhubarb and cook until tender, about 2 minutes. Remove the rhubarb from the syrup and set aside. Add the wine, vinegar, and cabbage strips to the syrup. Simmer for about 40 minutes.

Preheat oven to 400°F.

Meanwhile, cook the rice as directed on the packaging.

Cover the salmon with a bit of olive oil and sprinkle generously with salt and pepper. Bake for 15–20 minutes.

Take the cabbage out of the pan and mix it with the cooked black rice. Drizzle with a little of the remaining liquid from the pan.

Place the salmon on a platter with the sour cream and rhubarb. Serve the cabbage and rice mixture next to it.

THE SWEET

PIE WITH BAKED RHUBARB

DOUGH

1¼ cups flour
2 Tbsp icing sugar
½ cup cold butter
3 Tbsp water

RHUBARB

2¼ cups sliced rhubarb
Juice of 1 orange
¼ cup cane sugar

CREAM

1 vanilla pod
⅜ cup sugar
2 egg yolks
1¼ Tbsp cornstarch
⅔ cup milk
⅓ cup cream

Preheat oven to 400 °F.

Mix the flour and icing sugar together. Cut the butter into small cubes and crumble these into the flour until it develops a gritty consistency. Add the water and knead briefly into a dough. Refrigerate for at least 4 hours, preferably overnight. Blind bake in a 10-inch diameter pie dish for 15–20 minutes. Remove and reduce the oven temperature to 350°F.

Place the sliced rhubarb in a dish, and brush with the orange juice and sugar. Bake for 10 minutes until the pieces are tender but still keep their shape.

Split the vanilla pod and scrape out the seeds. Mix the seeds with the sugar. Add the egg yolks and cornstarch and mix thoroughly. In a pot, bring the milk and vanilla pod to a boil. Remove the pod from the pot and then add the egg mixture. Heat it until it thickens, then remove from heat. Refrigerate.

Whip the ⅓ cup of cream and mix it with the chilled cream mixture. Put the mixture on the bottom of the cooled pie crust and top with the rhubarb—you choose how artistic it should be. Garnish with wood sorrel and mint, if you like.

BLONDIE WITH PISTACHIOS

2 cups white chocolate, divided
1 cup butter
1 vanilla pod
1 cup sugar
½ cup flour
3 eggs
1½ cups salted pistachios
2 stalks rhubarb
A little liquid honey

Preheat oven to 350°F.

Melt 1½ cups of the chocolate over a water bath and melt the butter in a saucepan.

Split the vanilla pod and scrape out the seeds. Mix the sugar, flour, and vanilla seeds in a bowl, and beat the eggs into the mixture until slightly fluffy.

Scoop the butter and melted chocolate into the mixture with a dough scraper or similar.

Coarsely chop the pistachios and the last ½ cup of chocolate and fold these into the mixture. Place the dough in a baking tin lined with parchment paper.

Cut the rhubarb into long slices and lay these on top of the dough. Brush them with a bit of honey.

Bake the cake for about 50 minutes. (It's okay if a little comes to the surface when you fork test it.) Allow the cake to cool completely before cutting and eating.

SPRING MERINGUE WITH SKYR CREAM

MARINATED RHUBARB
3 rhubarb stalks
1 Tbsp pomegranate vinegar
3 Tbsp cane sugar
A little water
¼ cup pistachios

CREAM
1⅓ cup whipping cream
1 cup plain skyr or full-fat
   Greek yogurt
2 vanilla pods
2 Tbsp sugar

MERINGUE BASE
4 egg whites
1 cup sugar
1 cup coconut flour
¾ cup chopped dark chocolate

Preheat oven to 325°F.

Cut the rhubarb into pieces. Toss these in the vinegar and cane sugar and then place in a saucepan with a little water over medium heat. The rhubarb should be cooked until the pieces are a little tender but still have a bite to them. Take the pan off the heat and let the rhubarb cool.

Whip the egg whites and sugar together until completely stiff. Fold in the coconut flour and chocolate. Spread the meringue into the desired shape on a baking sheet and bake for about 25 minutes.

Whip the cream until foamy and gently fold it into the skyr. Split the vanilla pods and scrape out the seeds. Mix the seeds with the sugar to distribute them before folding them into the cream (if necessary, add a little extra sugar to taste).

Layer the cream onto the meringue base, then add the rhubarb, and finally top with chopped pistachios and a little extra chocolate.

RHUBARB CRUMBLE

SESAME SUGAR

¾ cup sesame seeds

¼ cup sugar

CRUMBLE

½ cup sugar

¾ cup flour

½ cup butter

1 cup oats

FILLING

2 cups cubed rhubarb

2 Tbsp sugar

1 Tbsp vanilla sugar

MINT DRESSING

¾ cup 18% sour cream

1 Tbsp cane sugar

Mint to taste

Preheat oven to 400°F.

Roast the sesame seeds in a dry pan over medium-low heat until golden. Toast the sugar in a saucepan over medium heat. When the sugar is golden, add the sesame seeds and mix well. Pour the sesame sugar out onto parchment paper and let cool.

Mix the crumble ingredients well. Break the sesame sugar into smaller pieces and add to the crumble mixture.

Toss the rhubarb in the sugar and vanilla sugar and place in an ovenproof dish. Break up the crumble dough into small pieces on top of the rhubarb and bake for about 25 minutes.

Mix the sour cream and cane sugar well. Finely chop the mint and stir in. Serve the mint dressing over the crumble.

PAVLOVA WITH RHUBARB

FILLING

2½ cups chopped rhubarb
½ cup cane sugar
1 Tbsp water
4 cups cream
2 tsp vanilla sugar
½ Tbsp icing sugar

MERINGUES

8 egg whites
2¾ cups sugar
3 tsp white wine vinegar
1 tsp vanilla sugar
A little icing sugar

Preheat oven to 250°F.

Bring the rhubarb, cane sugar, and water to a simmer in a saucepan and cook just until the rhubarb is tender. Let cool completely.

In a bowl, beat the egg whites to soft peaks. Add the sugar, little by little, while whipping at high speed. When half of the sugar has been added, whisk in the vinegar and vanilla sugar before beating in the rest of the sugar.

Sprinkle a little icing sugar on 2 pieces of parchment paper and divide the meringue between the two pieces. Shape each meringue into a circle with a small recess in the center. Bake in the oven for about 1½ hours.

Beat the cream and fold in the vanilla sugar and the ½ Tbsp of icing sugar. Once the meringues have cooled completely, assemble the cake: Layer half the cream on top of one meringue, then add half the rhubarb, then repeat with the second meringue, the remaining cream, and the remaining rhubarb.

SMALL MARZIPAN CAKES

½ cup flour
½ tsp baking powder
2 Tbsp blue poppy seeds
Pinch of salt
⅓ cup softened unsalted butter
½ cup cane sugar
1 egg
3 Tbsp sour cream
1 tsp vanilla extract
½ cup cubed rhubarb
¼ cup marzipan

Preheat oven to 350°F.

Mix the flour, baking powder, poppy seeds, and salt in a bowl.

In another bowl, beat together the butter and sugar. Add the egg, sour cream, and vanilla extract. Stir the flour mixture in gradually.

Add the rhubarb to the dough along with the marzipan (broken into small pieces) and stir gently.

Put the dough in small greased muffin tins and bake for about 20 minutes.

RHUBARB BANANA BREAD

1 cup butter
½ cup cane sugar
1 cup brown sugar
2 eggs
4 or 5 ripe bananas
⅓ cup whole milk
1½ cups wheat flour

¾ cup whole wheat flour
1½ tsp vanilla sugar
1 tsp baking powder
1¼ cups dark chocolate
½ cup almonds
5 small stalks of strawberry
    rhubarb

Preheat oven to 350°F.

Melt the butter and mix it with the sugars. Add the eggs. Mash the bananas thoroughly and mix them with the milk, before adding to the other bowl.

Combine the flours, vanilla sugar, and baking powder. Fold this into the wet mixture and combine thoroughly.

Coarsly chop the chocolate and almonds and fold these into the dough. Place the dough in a loaf tin.

Cut the rhubarb stalks to fit the tin. Press some of the rhubarb into the dough and place the rest on top.

Bake for about 50 minutes. Prick the bread with a skewer—the bread is done if no dough clings onto the skewer when you pull it up.

RHUBARB CHIPS

Cut rhubarb into long, thin strips. Bake in the oven at 150°F for about 7 hours until the strips are completely crispy.

Use the chips as a garnish on cakes or as a topping on skyr, yogurt, porridge, and the like.

A RHUBARB FARMER'S STORY

In the early autumn, I visited Lars Skytte at his farm on Funen, an island in my home country of Denmark. His farm is a 75-acre enterprise with an impressive history.

After an almost two-hour drive from Copenhagen to Årslev, I arrive at Skyttes Gartneri ("Shooter's Garden"). I knock on the door, and out comes a tall, smiling man in shorts and a short-sleeved shirt. Lars welcomes me, and within the first few minutes, I can feel his fervor burning through. I'm definitely visiting the right person.

Lars Skytte has cultivated his organic farm on Funen since 1983 and has been a pioneer of organic farming in Denmark since the 70s. Since the early 1990s, he has grown rhubarb and now delivers about 40–50,000 bundles a year to stores around the country. In other words, he is something of a rhubarb expert, and one with a great passion for what he does. He is also an incredibly welcoming character.

I now give the floor to the rhubarb farmer from Funen:

MY STORY

Right up to the 1960s, rhubarb was eaten almost daily in many Danish homes from mid-April until Midsummer's Day. Some may even remember being force-fed the fruity vegetable in porridge, gruel, and juice—the first hint of the approaching summer. Rhubarb used to hold a place our diet in the period between the previous year's winter apples and the coming season's summer apples. And with its high malic acid content, among other things, rhubarb constituted an appealing alternative in the transition between the fruits of each year.

When fruit imports increased during the 1960s and apples could be bought outside the Danish season, rhubarb—once a much-appreciated spring food—quickly slipped into the background. Rhubarb vanished almost entirely from the Danish market for the next three decades before being invited back again by far-sighted chefs, food writers, and gardeners in the late 1990s.

Botanically, rhubarb (Rheum rhaponticum) belongs to the buckwheat family, as do its wild relatives knotweed, sorrel, and dock. The plant is believed to originate in central Asia and first became known in Denmark in the mid-1700s.

Rhubarb is one of the plants that has been used for the widest variety of purposes in Danish cuisine. Rhubarb was introduced in Denmark as a medicinal plant in the 1700s. The root has been included in a wide range of remedies for various ailments; among other things, it has been used against scurvy, in cough remedies, and as a laxative. Right up to the 1940s, one could find prescriptions for arthritis treatment in which rhubarb drops were part of the medicine.

Even before that time, the root's yellow dye was known both by the people who used it to dye wool and by the clergy in England, where hair was dyed with it. Just read this recipe from the venerable master Alexis Piedmont's *The Secrets of Alexis of Piedmont*:

"To dye the hair golden as gold, the scrapings of a rhubarb root are taken and soaked in white wine. After washing your head with the mixture, wet the hair again with a sponge and let it dry in front of the fire or under the sun. After that, get it wet again and let it dry."

As a horticultural plant, it was not until the 1860s that rhubarb was introduced in some places in the country, and with great success. In fact, it is mentioned that, "it was the first trendy herb that found its way over the farmer's garden fence."

For the next hundred years, rhubarb was a treasured harbinger of spring and even managed to give its name to an entire neighborhood outside the city walls of Copenhagen. Before Vesterbro was built in the late 1800s, the gardeners close to Copenhagen grew vegetables just outside the city walls. The vegetables were sold in the markets inside the city during the day. One of the more nutrient-intensive crops grown was rhubarb. At that time, night soil was transported from the cities to the horticultural crops that needed it the most. And so the large, newly built working-class district Vesterbro was also known as the "Rhubarb Quarter," with a slightly condescending undertone.

GROW IT YOURSELF

When buying rhubarb plants for your garden, it's essential to know what you want since different varieties have significant differences in terms of taste, stalk size, color, germination time, and acid content. In the Danish clone collection at the experimental station in Årslev, there are more than 70 varieties of rhubarb, but not all varieties are equally interesting. However, the selection of rhubarb varieties at the Danish nurseries and garden centers is often very sparse, so finding the exact variety you want can be challenging.

Below, I will explain the different qualities of selected varieties.

Color

If you want rhubarb varieties that are very red, both outside and inside the stem, the varieties Svendborg Wine Rhubarb, Marshall's Early Red, and Elmsfeuer can be recommended. These varieties will all give a rich red color during cooking. Conversely, some varieties are almost colorless during cooking. These include Linnaeus and Timberley Early. The very red varieties will typically be 25–50 percent lower than the green varieties in yield. Attention should be paid to the fact that the group of dyes (anthocyanins) that give rhubarb its red color is very light-sensitive, so prepared foods should be stored in the dark.

Acidity

Previously it was thought that the high content of oxalic acid in rhubarb stalks caused kidney stones or even decalcification of the skeleton; however, this has not been substantiated. But one thing is sure; varieties with low oxalic acid content are generally considered to have a more pleasant mouthfeel. Several things are crucial when it comes to rhubarb's oxalic acid content:

- Variety differences. Timberley Early and Rosara are two varieties which contain relatively little oxalic acid, while Holsteiner Blut has a high acid content.
- The older the stalk becomes, the greater the oxalic acid content becomes. Therefore, if you want to reduce oxalic acid levels, you can choose to pick your stems while they are small and firm.
- The older the entire plant becomes, the lower the oxalic acid content becomes.

All this talk about oxalic acid may not matter much when it comes down to it, as oxalic acid has no bearing on taste. On the other hand, the content of malic acid does, which is another organic acid that appears in large quantities in rhubarb. In fact, it is malic acid that occurs in the most significant quantity.

Studies have found that when the amount of malic acid is between 18 and 22 percent of the dry weight of the stems, you get the ideal rhubarb flavor. If there is too little malic acid, the rhubarb flavor will disappear. If there is too much, the taste will be too sharp. Two varieties have made a special name for themselves with a good, stable taste; these are Marshall's Early Red and Spangsbjerg IIIS.

PLANTING

When planting your rhubarb seedlings, it is essential to dig a deep hole so that the sod is loosened deeper than the tuber. Here, the soil can be mixed with good compost before putting the plant on top at the level of the soil's surface. If you plant in the autumn, it is usually unnecessary to water, but if you are planting in spring, you should pay attention to the water balance. After planting, the rhubarb plant must not be disturbed for the following year to gain proper hold and form a new root network.

In the first year, it is important to carry out weed control, but once the plant is established, the need for this decreases since rhubarb, with its early, aggressive growth, is good at suppressing invasive plants and their attempts at competition. However, root weeds such as quick grass, ground elder, and creeping thistle must be controlled thoroughly throughout the year.

Rhubarb is a perennial that uses the growing season to gather next year's growth supplies. Therefore, it is important not to over-harvest your plant when taking pickings for your kitchen. Finally, the rhubarb stalks must not be cut off but must be pulled up instead, to ensure that new stalks will continue to grow. It is important to pull only one stalk at a time and to pull sideways to protect the plant as much as possible and avoid pulling up the nodes. You will also get more of the white, juicy part at the base of the stalk by doing this.

It is generally recommended to stop harvesting rhubarb around Midsummer's Day. This rule is excellent for young plants that have not yet established a large tuber to store nutrition in. However, if you have some older tubers that you haven't picked from too much in the early summer, you can easily harvest rhubarb stalks over the summer and post-summer, as long as you leave about 75 percent of the stalks intact. Stalks harvested in late summer usually are not of the same quality as the spring stalks. But in a rainy summer, you may well get satisfactory results.

COMPOTE

RHUBARB COMPOTE
WITH GINGER

3 Tbsp fresh ginger
5 cups chopped rhubarb
1 cup cane sugar
1 tsp sodium benzoate (optional)

Peel the ginger and cut it finely. Put all ingredients in a saucepan.
Cook over medium-low heat until it becomes a thick compote.

RHUBARB COMPOTE
WITH MINT

1 small handful of fresh mint
5 cups chopped rhubarb
1¼ cups cane sugar
1 tsp sodium benzoate (optional)

Chop the mint. Place all ingredients in a saucepan. Cook over
medium-low heat until it becomes a thick compote.

RHUBARB COMPOTE WITH VANILLA

1 vanilla pod
5 cups chopped rhubarb
1¼ cups cane sugar
1 tsp sodium benzoate (optional)

Scrape the vanilla seeds out of the pod. Put all the ingredients in a pot—including the vanilla pod. Cook over medium-low heat until it becomes a thick compote.

JARRING & STORAGE

All three compotes must cool down a bit before being put in hot glasses that have optionally been rinsed with sodium benzoate. Each compote recipe makes enough to fill one 24 oz (750 mL) glass jar.

Store in a dark, cool cupboard before opening and in the refrigerator after opening. The shelf life is approximately 3 months before opening and 1 week after opening.

All three compotes can be used in the subsequent recipes, according to your preferences.

OVERNIGHT PORRIDGE

1⅓ cups Greek yogurt
¾ cup almond milk
½ cup rhubarb compote (see pages 62–64)
1⅓ cups oats

Mix all ingredients well and refrigerate overnight.

Optional garnishes can include blue poppy seeds, chopped nuts, a little extra compote, rhubarb chips (see page 46), or a little extra almond milk.

RHUBARB SANDWICH COOKIES

Makes 16 small, round cookies each 2½ inches in diameter

DOUGH

2½ cups wheat flour
Pinch of salt
1 tsp cardamom
1 cup unsalted butter
1¼ cups icing sugar
1 egg
1 Tbsp vanilla sugar

ICING

1 egg white
Icing sugar
1 drop vinegar
16 tsp (approx. ½ cup)
 rhubarb compote
 (see pages 62–64)

Mix the wheat flour, salt, and cardamom together. Cut the butter into small cubes and crumble it into the flour until it reaches a uniform, gritty consistency. Add the icing sugar, egg, and vanilla sugar, and knead the dough together quickly. Wrap the dough and refrigerate for 1 hour.

Preheat the oven to 375°F.

Roll out the dough to a thickness of about ⅛ inch. Cut out small circles with a round cookie cutter, a glass, or something similar, and place them on a baking sheet lined with parchment paper.

Bake the cookies for about 10 minutes until slightly golden. Cool on a baking rack.

To make the icing, beat the icing sugar, little by little, into the egg white, and continue until you have a toothpaste-like consistency. Whip the vinegar in at the end.

Ice 8 of the cookies and place 1 teaspoon of compote on each of the other 8. Then, layer an icing cookie on top of each compote cookie and gently press them together. If desired, garnish with pieces of rhubarb chips (see page 46).

CHEESECAKE

BASE

30 digestive biscuits
¾ cup butter

FILLING

5 leaves of gelatine
2 vanilla pods
1¾ cups cream cheese
1 cup sour cream
½ cup sugar
Juice of 1 unsprayed lime
½ cup rhubarb compote
    (see pages 62–64)

Preheat the oven to 400°F.

Soak the gelatine leaves in cold water.

Blend the biscuits into a flour, and melt the butter. Mix the biscuit
flour and butter together and press the mixture into the bottom of a
springform pan. Bake for 10 minutes.

Split the vanilla pods and the scrape the seeds out. Combine the cream
cheese, sour cream, sugar, and vanilla until thoroughly blended.

Wring out the gelatine leaves and melt them in a little (approx. 2½ Tbsp)
just-boiled water. Pour the lime juice and a little of the cheesecake mixture
into the gelatine water to temper it. Then add the rest of the cheesecake
mixture and combine.

Put the cheesecake mixture on top of the base and knock out any air
bubbles. Add the rhubarb compote on top in small dollops. Then gently
stir the compote into the cheesecake mixture with a chopstick or similar
to create a marbled effect.

Refrigerate the cake for at least 4 hours or preferably overnight.
If desired, decorate with rhubarb chips before serving (see page 46).

TRIFLE

The quantities below serve 1 person. Multiply as needed for your group.

3 Tbsp whipped cream
4 small macaroons
4 Tbsp rhubarb compote (see pages 62–64)
Dark chocolate

Whip the cream and crush the macaroons.

Assemble each trifle in a small glass, starting with the compote on the bottom, then the crushed macaroons, then the whipped cream. Grate a little chocolate on top.

PANCAKES

Makes 8–10 pancakes

DOUGH
1 cup flour
¼ cup coconut flour (desiccated coconut)
1 Tbsp blue poppy seeds
2 tsp baking powder
3 Tbsp sugar
2 tsp vanilla sugar
¾ cup milk
1 egg
1 Tbsp lime juice
Salt

GARNISH
Rhubarb compote (see pages 62–64)
Skyr or full-fat Greek yogurt

Mix all the ingredients for the dough together thoroughly and fry into pancakes in a hot pan.

Top with compote and a little skyr.

CHUTNEY & RELISH

RHUBARB CHUTNEY

1-pint (500 mL) glass jar

2 onions
2½ cups chopped rhubarb
⅓ cup white wine
⅔ cup apple cider vinegar
¾ cup sugar
2 tsp yellow mustard seeds
2 tsp ground cloves
½ tsp cumin seeds
1 chili
3 tablespoons fresh ginger
Salt and pepper

Cut the onion into thin slices and mix with the rhubarb.

Place all the ingredients in a saucepan and boil for about 15 minutes, until the rhubarb is cooked all the way through.

Let the chutney cool a little before putting it in a hot glass jar.* Store in a dark, cool cupboard, and refrigerate after opening. The shelf life is approximately 3 months before opening and 1 week after opening.

*The glass can be rinsed first in sodium benzoate, if you choose.

Ingefær og Chili
Rabarber Chutney

GREEN SALAD WITH GRILLED ASPARAGUS

½ pound asparagus
1 avocado
½ cucumber
1 cup shelled edamame beans
¾ cup snap peas
½ bunch spring onions
1½ cups mâche (lamb's lettuce)
½ cup goat's cheese
4 Tbsp rhubarb chutney (see page 78)

Break the asparagus spears and discard the ends. Grill the asparagus in a dry pan.

Halve the avocado, take it out of the peel, and cut into slices. Assemble the rest of the vegetables and cut into smaller pieces, if necessary.

Place the vegetables in a large dish and top with crumbled goat's cheese and the rhubarb chutney.

BAKED BRIE

¼ cup almonds
¼ cup hazelnuts
1 Tbsp honey
1 wheel of brie
Rhubarb chutney (see page 78)

Preheat oven to 400°F.

Coarsely chop the nuts and mix with the honey.

Place the brie on a baking sheet lined with parchment paper and put the nuts on top. Bake for 15–20 minutes until the cheese is soft inside.

Serve with bread or crackers and rhubarb chutney.

RHUBARB RELISH

1 half-pint (250 mL) glass jar

2 stalks rhubarb
1 onion
⅓ cup white vinegar
⅓ cup apple cider vinegar
½ cup sugar
1 tsp yellow mustard seeds
Salt and pepper, to taste

Cut the rhubarb into long, thin strips. Cut the onion into fine, thin slices and mix with the rhubarb. Warm the vinegars, sugar, mustard seeds, salt, and pepper on the stove. When the sugar is dissolved, add the onion and rhubarb. Simmer for 10–15 minutes until the rhubarb is completely tender.

Let the relish cool a little before putting it into a hot glass jar.* Store in a dark, cool cupboard, and refrigerate after opening. The shelf life is approximately 3 months before opening and 1 week after opening.

*The glass can be rinsed first in sodium benzoate, if you choose.

Rabarber
Relish

PULLED PORK BURGERS

MEAT

⅓ cup brown sugar
2 Tbsp sweet paprika
2 Tbsp smoked paprika
2 Tbsp onion powder
2 Tbsp cumin
1 Tbsp chili flakes
1 Tbsp garlic powder
1 Tbsp coarse sea salt
5-pound pork collar

Mix all seasoning ingredients together and rub into the meat thoroughly. Wrap the meat and refrigerate for at least 2 hours, preferably overnight.

Slow roast the pork collar at 200°F. The time depends on the size and thickness; check the packaging if necessary. Alternatively, use a roast thermometer: when the core temperature reaches 158–167°F, it is ready.

(continued on next page)

BURGER BUNS

⅔ cup whole milk
2½ Tbsp yeast
¼ cup sugar
4¼ cups flour
3 eggs
2 tsp salt
½ cup softened butter

Warm the milk up to 95°F and dissolve the yeast and sugar in it. Sift the flour into the milk, half at a time, and stir well between each half.

Add the eggs one at a time while kneading the dough. Add the salt and butter and continue kneading. If necessary, add more flour until the dough releases from the edges of the bowl.

Knead the dough for 10 minutes and let it rise for about 1 hour in a covered bowl until it has doubled in size.

Shape into 8 buns, lay them out on a baking sheet, and leave to rise for about 40 minutes. Preheat the oven to 350°F. Brush the buns with a beaten egg or milk and bake for about 15 minutes.

TOPPINGS

Your choice of greens
Mayonnaise
Rhubarb relish (see page 84)

Assemble the burgers with the slow-roasted meat, greens, mayonnaise, and rhubarb relish.

SPICY HOT DOGS

4 cherry tomatoes
1 small red onion
1 avocado
1 small handful of cilantro
4 hot dogs
4 hot dog buns
Tortilla chips, crumbled
Jalapeños (optional)
4 Tbsp rhubarb relish (see page 84)

Cut the tomatoes, onions, and avocados into slices. Coarsely chop the cilantro.

Fry the hot dogs over medium heat. Heat the buns. Place the hot dogs in the buns and top with sliced vegetables, the tortilla chips, jalapeños, and rhubarb relish.

DRINKS

RHUBARB GIN

1.5-pint (750 mL) glass bottle

5 cups chopped rhubarb
2¼ cups sugar
3 cups (750 mL) gin
1 tsp sodium benzoate (optional)

Wash the rhubarb and cut it into pieces of about 1½ inches. Place in a hot glass bottle,* along with the sugar, and refrigerate the bottle.

After 24 hours, add the gin. Store the bottle in a dark, cold place for 4 weeks. During the first week, shake the bottle well at least once daily.

Remove the rhubarb from the gin by pouring it over a strainer into a clean jug. Then transfer the gin into a new bottle or bottles.

*The glass bottle can be rinsed first with sodium benzoate if you choose.

G&T

Ice
1 part rhubarb gin (see page 94)
2 parts tonic

Fill the glass with ice. Add the rhubarb gin and tonic.

LIGHT & STORMY

Ice
1½ oz (50 mL) rhubarb gin (see page 94)
⅓ oz (10 mL) lime juice
3½ oz (100 mL) ginger beer

Fill the glass with ice. Add the rhubarb gin, lime juice, and ginger beer.

RHUBARB JUICE WITH VANILLA

1 quart (1 L) jar

6 cups water
5 cups chopped rhubarb
2 vanilla pods
2¼ cups cane sugar
Lime juice (optional)

Bring the water, rhubarb, and vanilla pods to a quick boil. Turn down the heat and let simmer for 10 minutes. Remove the pan from the heat and let sit for 30 minutes.

Pour the juice through a strainer into another saucepan and add the sugar. Let it boil until the sugar is dissolved. Add lime juice (optional) and extra sugar to taste.

Let the juice cool slightly before putting it in a hot glass bottle.* Store in the refrigerator.

When serving, mix the juice with water at a ratio of 1 part juice to 3 parts water.

*The glass bottle can be rinsed first with sodium benzoate if you choose.

RHUBARB MULE

Ice
1½ oz (45 mL) vodka
2 slices of cucumber
1 oz (30 mL) rhubarb juice (see page 100)
½ cup ginger beer

Fill the glass ⅔ of the way with ice. Add vodka and cucumber.
Add the rhubarb juice and stir. Top with ginger beer.

CORIANDER SMASH

2 large slices/wedges of unsprayed lime
1 small handful of cilantro
1 oz (30 mL) vodka
¾ oz (22 mL) rhubarb juice (see page 100)
2 oz (60 mL) sparkling water
Ice

Mash the lime and cilantro together in a container.

Add vodka and mash again thoroughly.

Add rhubarb juice, along with the sparkling water, and stir.
Strain into a glass with ice

REFERENCES

A. Thuesen. State plant growing experiments. *Variety rating of rhubarb 1977–79*. Notice no. 1640.

Kaj Henriksen and Gitte Bjørn. *Growing rhubarb*. Green knowledge, No. 158. March 2004.

Kimmo Rumpunen and Kaj Henriksen. *Phytochemical and morphological characterization of seventy-one cultivars and selections of culinary rhubarb*. Journal of Horticultural Science and Biotechnology. 1999.

Kimmo Rumpunen. *Rhubarb – a robust culture*. Garden Fact Sheet, No. 12. 1996.

V.J. Brøndegaard. *People and Flora – Danish ethnobotany*. Rosenkilde and Bagger. 1978.

ACKNOWLEDGMENTS

A big thank you to the friends and family who have helped with the creation of this book. Your help is invaluable.

Thanks to Lars Skytte, who has shared his knowledge of rhubarb so that both the readers and I could become wiser.

Thanks to Broste Copenhagen, Trine Rytter Ceramics, Vildersbøll, KH Würtz, Pillivuyt, and Luigi Bormioli for lending the most beautiful workspaces.

Thanks to artist and designer Marianne Foersom for the beautiful backgrounds.

INDEX

ABOUT THE AUTHOR

Since 2013, Søren Staun Petersen has created recipes focusing on seasonal fruits and vegetables on Chef's Season and developed recipes for brands and magazines. By virtue of his work as a professional commercial photographer, mainly focusing on food photography, he has worked with food and its presentation for several years. Søren has a great passion for fresh Danish ingredients. In August 2018, Søren published his first cookbook, *Surprise with Pumpkin*.

FIRST ENGLISH-LANGUAGE EDITION

Originally published in Denmark in 2019 by Muusmann Forlag, Copenhagen, as *Rabarber: nye og klassiske opskrifter til salt og sødt* (ISBN 9788793679443)

Recipes and photography © 2018 by Søren Staun Petersen
English translation © 2022 by Natalie Pitu

TouchWood Editions
touchwoodeditions.com

The information in this book is true and complete to the best of the author's knowledge. All recommendations are made without guarantee on the part of the author or the publisher.

Cover and interior design by Lara Minja
Photo on page 5 by Martin Bjørn Christiansen

CATALOGUING DATA AVAILABLE FROM LIBRARY AND ARCHIVES CANADA

ISBN 9781771514040 (softcover)
ISBN 9781771514057 (electronic)

TouchWood Editions acknowledges that the land on which we live and work is within the traditional territories of the Lkwungen (Esquimalt and Songhees), Malahat, Pacheedaht, Scia'new, T'Sou-ke and W̱SÁNEĆ (Pauquachin, Tsartlip, Tsawout, Tseycum) peoples.

We acknowledge the financial support of the Government of Canada through the Canada Book Fund and of the Province of British Columbia through the Book Publishing Tax Credit.

This book was produced using FSC®-certified, acid-free papers, processed chlorine free, and printed with soya-based inks.

Printed in China

27 26 25 24 23 1 2 3 4 5

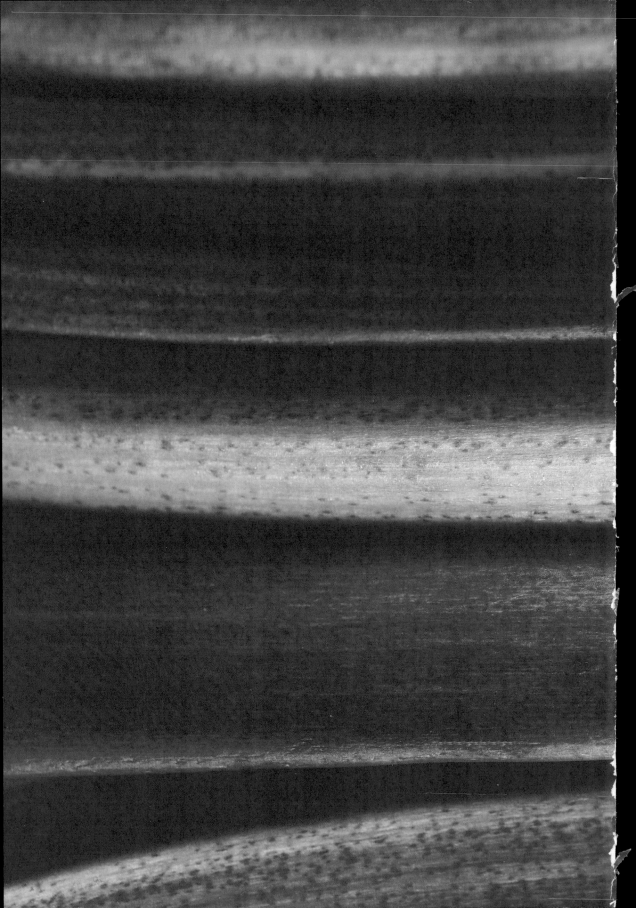